SPORTS
STARTERS

Smash it Tennis

Paul Challen

 Crabtree Publishing Company

www.crabtreebooks.com

SPORTS STARTERS

Created by Bobbie Kalman

Author
Paul Challen

Project coordinator
Kathy Middleton

Editors
Janine Belzak
Molly Aloian
Rachel Stuckey

Photo research
Melissa McClellan

Design
Tibor Choleva
Melissa McClellan

Production coordinator
Ken Wright

Prepress technician
Ken Wright

Illustrations
Leif Peng: page 9

Photographs
David McHutchison: back cover; pages 1, 3, 6, 11, 12, 13, 15, 17, 18,
    20, 21, 22, 23, 29, 31 (top right),
Melissa McClellan: page 28
Shutterstock.com: pages 5, 16, 18, 26, 27, 30, 31
iStockphoto.com: cover; pages 4, 7, 10, 14, 24
Photofusion, photographersdirect.com: page 19

Special thanks to
Hannah Lange, Sadie Lange, Sandee Ewasiuk,
Flora Karsai of Ontario Tennis Association,
David Lea of Ontario Tennis Association,
and David McHutchison

Created for Crabtree Publishing by Silver Dot Publishing

Library and Archives Canada Cataloguing in Publication

Challen, Paul, 1967-
    Smash it tennis / Paul Challen.

(Sports starters)
Includes index.
ISBN 978-0-7787-3145-0 (bound).--ISBN 978-0-7787-3177-1 (pbk.)

    1. Tennis--Juvenile literature. I. Title. II. Series: Sports starters
(St. Catharines, Ont.)

GV996.5.C43 2010   j796.342   C2009-906938-5

Library of Congress Cataloging-in-Publication Data

Challen, Paul C. (Paul Clarence), 1967-
  Smash it tennis / Paul Challen.
       p. cm. -- (Sports starters)
  Includes index.
  ISBN 978-0-7787-3177-1 (pbk. : alk. paper) -- ISBN 978-0-7787-3145-0
(reinforced library binding : alk. paper)
  1. Tennis--Juvenile literature. I. Title. II. Series.

  GV996.5.C43 2010
  796.342--dc22

                                                    2009048050

Crabtree Publishing Company

www.crabtreebooks.com   1-800-387-7650

Printed in the U.S.A./122009/CG20091120

Published in Canada
Crabtree Publishing
616 Welland Ave.
St. Catharines, Ontario
L2M 5V6

Published in the United States
Crabtree Publishing
PMB 59051
350 Fifth Avenue, 59th Floor
New York, New York 10118

Published in the United Kingdom
Crabtree Publishing
Maritime House
Basin Road North, Hove
BN41 1WR

Published in Australia
Crabtree Publishing
386 Mt. Alexander Rd.
Ascot Vale (Melbourne)
VIC 3032

Contents

What is tennis?

Tennis is a sport played both indoors and outdoors on a surface called a **court**. A court is made of grass, clay, or human-made materials. When one player plays another in tennis, it is called a **singles match**. When two players team up to play another pair of players, it is called a **doubles match**.

The court is made up of a playing surface, lines, and a net, as well as stands for the fans!

These players are playing singles tennis—a match between two players.

Back and forth

Players hit a ball over a net toward their opponents using a piece of equipment called a **racket**. When the ball flies back and forth over the net, it is called a **rally**. The ball can bounce on the court no more than once each time it crosses the net.

Gearing up

Tennis players do not need a lot of equipment. Comfortable shoes that you can run around in are a must. It is also important to wear comfortable clothes, such as shorts or track pants, and a t-shirt.

On the ball

Tennis balls are specially made to have a good bounce. Players keep a few tennis balls on hand when they play.

Comfort is important when choosing clothing for tennis

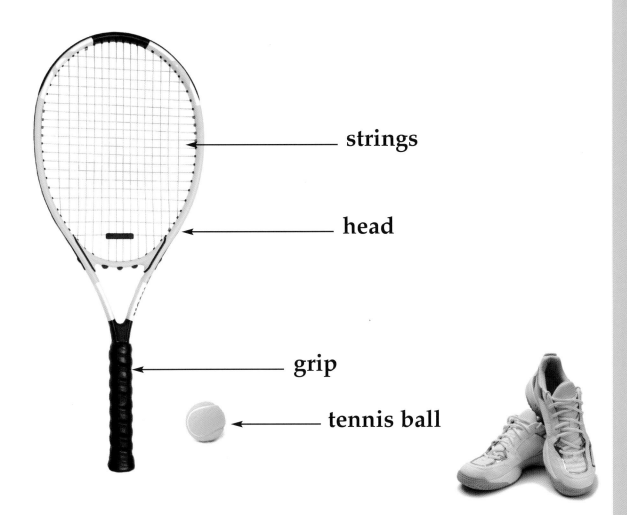

strings

head

grip

tennis ball

Making a racket

A tennis player uses a tennis racket to hit the ball.
A racket has a frame made of hard material, with
a loop at the end, called the **head**. The loop has
strings stretched across it from left to right and top to
bottom. When you swing the racket, the ball bounces
off the strings. At the other end of the racket there is a
grip, which lets you hold onto the racket comfortably.

Court date

There are lines around the outside of the tennis court in a rectangular shape. Balls must bounce inside or on these lines to keep the rally going. The lines at the back end of the court are called **baselines**. The lines at the side of the court are called **sidelines**.

Lined up

There are different lines on the outside of the court for singles and doubles matches. This is because doubles players need a wider court to play in. There are also special lines on the court showing players where they can **serve** the ball.

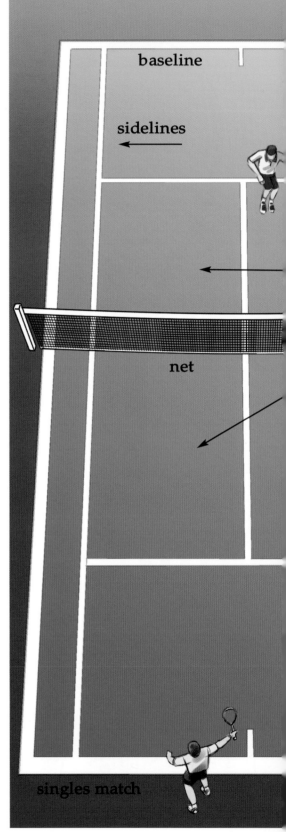

baseline

sidelines

net

singles match

sidelines

service
boxes

Net gains

Every tennis court is divided in half by a net.
Tennis nets have white material across the top.
This helps players see the top of the net clearly.

doubles match

Service!

Every game of tennis is made up of a series of **points**. The same player serves throughout an entire game, but points can be scored if a player is serving or receiving the ball. A player serving must hit the ball into an area on the opponent's side called the **service box** without hitting the net. When one player serves, his or her opponent tries to hit the ball back with a shot called a **return**.

Overhand serve

In an overhand serve, a player grips the racket at the end, and tosses the ball high in the air. At the ball's highest point, the server tries to hit the ball with his or her racket so that it travels down and into the opponent's service box.

A server needs accuracy and power to hit an ace.

Whose fault is it?

If the server hits the ball into the net, or misses the service box, it is called a fault. After a fault, the server gets another try. If he or she misses the second serve, it is called a double fault, and the server loses the point. If a player serves the ball into the opponent's service area and the other player does not touch it with his or her racket, it is called an ace.

Fantastic forehands

One of the most common shots in tennis is the **forehand** shot. Players hit the forehand shot on the same side of their body as the hand they are using to swing their racket. As the ball approaches, the player pulls the racket back in a motion called the **backswing**. He or she then swings the racket forward, hitting the ball with a smooth motion.

The easiest forehand grip is to hold the racket so the face is flat as the ball comes toward it.

Basic shot

Many players find the forehand to be the easiest shot to learn. A forehand shot or other shot that you hit without the ball first touching the court is called a **volley**.

When hitting a forehand, the ball will travel in the same direction as a player's feet are pointing.

13

Backing it up

A player sometimes has to reach across the body to hit a shot on the opposite side of the racket. This shot is called the **backhand shot**. To hit a backhand, the player must twist the body in the direction the ball will go. Players can hit a backhand with one hand or two hands.

Players use the one-handed backhand for accuracy.

A tough shot

It sounds tough to hit a backhand—and it can be. But learning and mastering the backhand is a great way to improve at tennis, because it forces players to reach many of those hard-to-get shots!

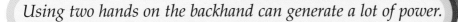

Using two hands on the backhand can generate a lot of power.

Smash it!

One of the most exciting shots in a tennis match is the **overhead smash**. The smash looks a lot like a serve. A player uses this shot to return a high shot hit by his or her opponent. Players hit the overhead smash when the ball is high over their head.

Power plus skill equals a good overhead smash.

All in the technique

To hit a smash, a player grips the racket at the end in the same grip used when serving. The player approaches the ball, and positions the feet in the direction he or she wants the ball to go. When the ball is at its highest point, the player brings the racket down quickly, aiming the ball down toward the opponent's court.

The smash is also effective in doubles.

Double trouble

In a doubles match, two players face off against two other players. When one team is serving, the server stands at the service line, just like in singles. His or her partner stands closer to the net. After each point, the server and his or her partner switch sides.

Right back to you!

The team that is returning serve sets up so that the player returning the serve stands on the baseline. His or her partner stands on the opposite side of the court.

Talk it up!

Doubles partners always have to be communicating with one another. They must know who is going to stand near the net, who is going to play at the baseline, and which half of the court is going to be covered by whom.

Teamwork is important in doubles matches.

Using a plan

Singles tennis players use different **strategies** to win points. Some players stay close to the baseline. They use forehand and backhand shots to hit the ball deep into their opponent's side. These players often hit the ball as close to the boundary lines as possible, and into the corners to make these shots hard to return.

Baseline players use deep, accurate shots to keep opponents guessing.

To the net!

Other players prefer to stay close to the net. As soon as their shots cross the net, these players are there to pounce on the ball and smash it back! But a well-placed lob—a high, arcing, or curving, shot over an opponent's head—can be a good way to get it past a player close to the net.

Keeping close to the net makes it hard for an opponent to return shots.

Keeping score

At the start of each game, both players have zero points. In tennis, zero is called **love**. Then when one player scores a point, he or she has 15 points. A second point moves the player to 30. On a third point, the player has 40. When a player scores a fourth point, he or she wins the game.

Keeping score adds excitement to a game.

Margin of victory

A player has to win a game by two points, so when the score is tied 40-40, or 40-all, one player must win two points in a row. When the score is tied at 40-all, it is called **deuce**. When a player wins one of the two points needed to win a game, it is called **advantage**.

Game, set, match!
Opponents play a series of games, called a set, with the first player to win six games winning the set. The first player to win either two or three sets wins the match.

Making it official

Tennis **officials** enforce the rules and make decisions about scoring. The **umpire** calls balls "in" or "out" depending on where they fall. The umpire also sorts out any arguments between players. **Line judges** and **net judges** help the umpire by deciding if the ball has touched the lines or the net during a serve.

The umpire sits high above the court to get a good view.

Keep them bouncing

In competitive tennis, ball boys and ball girls help the players by running after balls that have been hit into the net or outside the court. They toss balls back to players, making sure they always have enough balls to play with.

Ball boys and girls help keep the action moving.

Competition

In a tennis tournament, players take on one another in singles or doubles matches. Usually, the winning player or pair moves on to face another match winner, while the losers are **eliminated**. These elimination matches continue until there are only two players or doubles pairs left. They face off in the final, with the winner being declared winner of the tournament.

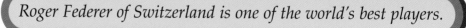
Roger Federer of Switzerland is one of the world's best players.

Around the world

Big tournaments around the world include the French, Australian, and US Opens, Wimbledon, and the Olympics. Among the top players in the world, there is a ranking system that tells fans of the sport how their favorite players compare to all the other best players.

Rafael Nadal of Spain, and sisters Venus and Serena Williams of the United States are always among the highest-ranked players in any tournament.

Mind your manners!

Tennis has important rules that make sure players get along with one another on the court, and help keep everyone safe and happy. Often, singles or doubles tennis is played without an umpire, so it is up to the players to agree on the rules and to act politely toward one another.

There is no place for arguing with an opponent in tennis.

Getting along

For example, the player closest to the ball has the right to call the ball "in" or "out" when it is close to the line. Players agree that the player calling the shot will be honest, and will not make an incorrect call just because it helps him or her. This is just one example of tennis **etiquette**.

Good sportsmanship is a big part of the game.

Smash it up!

You can find a lot of places to play tennis. Local clubs are usually happy to have young members, who can take lessons there to improve their game.

Tennis benefits

Tennis is a great way to stay fit because there is a lot of running. Tennis also helps with coordination because you are moving both your arms and feet to get in position to make shots and to hit the ball.

Get out and have fun playing tennis!

Glossary

Note: Boldfaced words that are defined in the text may not appear in the glossary

backhand A shot hit on the opposite side of a player's racket hand

court The lined surface on which a tennis game is played

doubles match A tennis match played by two players against two others

eliminated Getting knocked out of a tournament

etiquette The rules that make sure players in a tennis match treat each other fairly

forehand A shot hit on the same side as a player's racket hand

point The basic unit of scoring in tennis

racket The piece of equipment tennis players use to hit the ball

rally A series of back-and-forth shots that make up a point

return A shot in which one player hits another player's shot back over the net

serve The start of a point in tennis, in which a player throws a ball in the air and hits it over the net

service box The area in which a legal serve must fall

singles match A tennis match between two players

strategies A tennis player's plans for winning a game

Index